Sumário

#	Section	Page
1	About Me	5
2	People	6
3	Family	7
4	Food	8
5	Colors	12
6	Shapes	13
7	Characteristics	14
8	Toys	16
9	Clothes And Accessories	18
10	So Many Objects!	20
11	Sports	26
12	People We Know	30
13	Halloween	34
14	Christmas	35

Disney My First Pictionary

About Me

My name is
Meu nome é

I am a ☐ boy ☐ girl
Eu sou   menino   menina

I am ____ years old. I was born in ____
Eu tenho   anos de idade.   Eu nasci em

I live in a ☐ house ☐ apartment ☐ farm
Eu vivo em   casa   apartamento   fazenda

in the city of
na cidade de

with my ☐ parents ☐ siblings ☐ grandparents ☐ tutors
com meus   pais   irmãos   avós   tutores

I study at
Onde estudo

and I am on the ____ th grade.
e estou cursando a   série.

My favourite teacher is
Meu/ Minha professor/a favorito/a é

My best friend is
Meu/ Minha melhor amigo/a é

Things I like:
Coisas que eu gosto:

Things I don't like:
Coisas que eu não gosto:

2 People

boy

girl

man

woman

old

young

adult   child

Family 3

husband
Parents
wife

Children

sister

father
son
mother
daughter

brother

baby brother

Siblings

4 Food

orange

raspberries

zucchini

peach

mango

corn

brussel sprouts

lime

eggplant

blueberry

coconut

radish

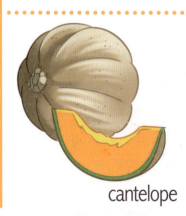
cantelope

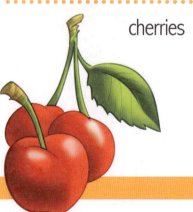
cherries

4 Food

steak

salad

spaghetti and meatballs

fish

water

roasted chicken

apple juice

spinach

loaf of bread

sandwich

soup

5 Colors

Primary Colors
- red
- blue
- yellow

Secondary Colors
- orange
- purple
- green

Neutral Colors
- black
- white
- gray

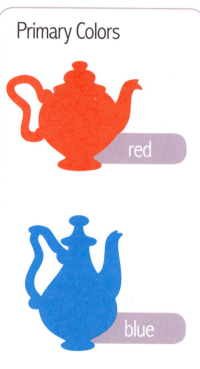

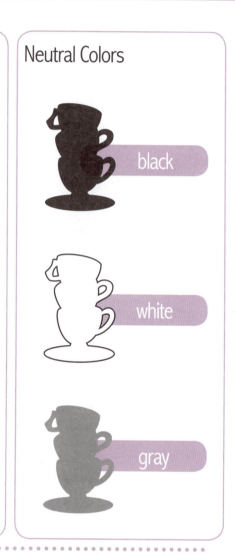

- pink
- ocre
- brown

- dark green
- dark blue
- light green
- light blue

Shapes 6

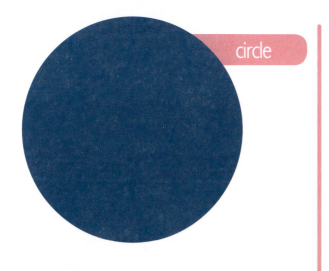
circle

square

hexagon

rectangle

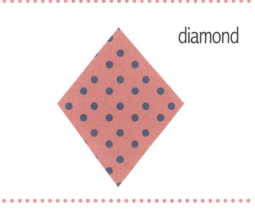
diamond

oval

pentagon

star

7 Characteristics

Hair Color

blonde

brunette

red-haired

Eye-color

green-eyed

brown-eyed

blue-eyed

14

Age

Height · Weight

8 Toys

robot

whirlgig

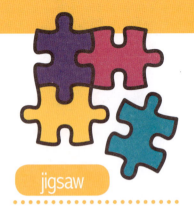
jigsaw

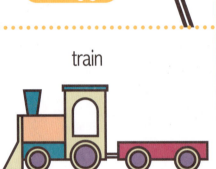
train

paper plane

rattle

rocking horse

kite

boat

spinning top

balloon

teddy bear

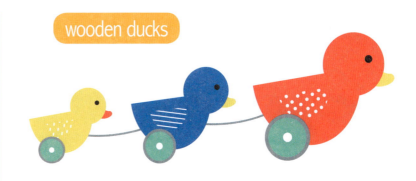
wooden ducks

beach ball

blocks

rubber duck

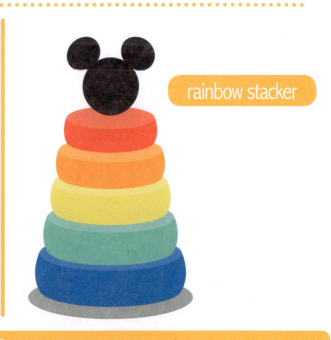
rainbow stacker

9 Clothes And Accessories

flip-flops

sunglasses

top hat

cap

knit cap

bathing suit

backpack

shoes

mitten

t-shirt

socks

hat

high heels

bow

18

purse

pants

skirt

shorts

sneakers

bib

button

scarf

blouse

shirt

boots

dress

bracelet

jacket

19

10 So Many Objects!

watering can

honey pot

keychain

Gardening Tools

shovel
fork

watch

tickets

key

passport

perfume

lipstick

rope

bowling pin

magnifier

camera

newspaper

paper lanterns

suitcase

20

telescope

fireworks

headphones

treasure map

tent

telephone

teapot

cup

tub

circus tent

compass

ship

21

10 So Many Objects!

door

scuba mask
snorkel

clock

window

lifesaver

castle

net

anchor

Card Suits

 clubs   hearts   spades   diamonds

fan

table

broom

rocking chair

armchair

lighthouse

chair

pencil

notebook

tray

mirror

couch

books

picture frame

23

10 So Many Objects!

kitchen scale

cake plate

rocket

bucket

up

right

down

left

candlestick

thread

screwdriver

wrench

shelf

24

 bed

 skull

 chest

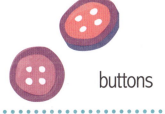 buttons

house

 toaster

 helmet

 lamp

 light bulb

 trash can

 television

 coins

 leash

11 Sports

karate

basketball

fitness

baseball glove

trophy

silver medal

volleyball

football

baseball

soccer ball

basketball

tennis racquet

gold medal

hiking

sailing

26

snowboarding
skiing
skis
table tennis

tennis

fishing

fishing rod

golfing

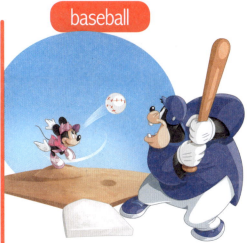
baseball

surfboard

surfing

football

12 People We Know

captain

police officer

singer

sailor

doctor

ballerina

cook

nurse

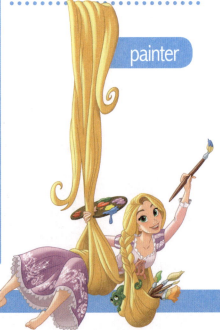
painter

shoemaker

astronaut

photographer

cheerleaders

waitress

queen

firefighters

king

31

12 People We Know

cowboy
cowgirl

pirate

mayor

seamstress

dressmaker

car racer

soccer player

maestro

sheriff

fairies

swordsperson

teacher

student

boy scout

traffic cop

musician

reader

13 Halloween

witch

ghost

mummy

Frankenstein's monster

vampire

Christmas 14

garland

ornament

christmas gift

santa's hat

santa claus

candy cane

christmas tree

35

15 Music

xylophone

tambourine

guitar

trumpet

bell

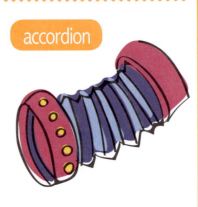
accordion

flute

castanets

electric guitar

guitar pick

violin

band

piano

musical notes

record

horn

drums

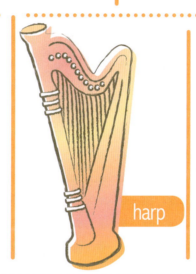
harp

drum

tuba

record player

16 Animals

white shark

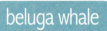
beluga whale

sea jelly

whale

seal

crab

sea lion

dolphin

fish

octopus

16 Animals

pig

jaguar

chipmunk

hippopotamus

elephant

koala

hedgehog

hyena

badger

tiger

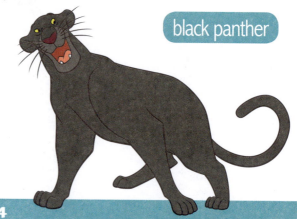
black panther

44

This Is My Body 17

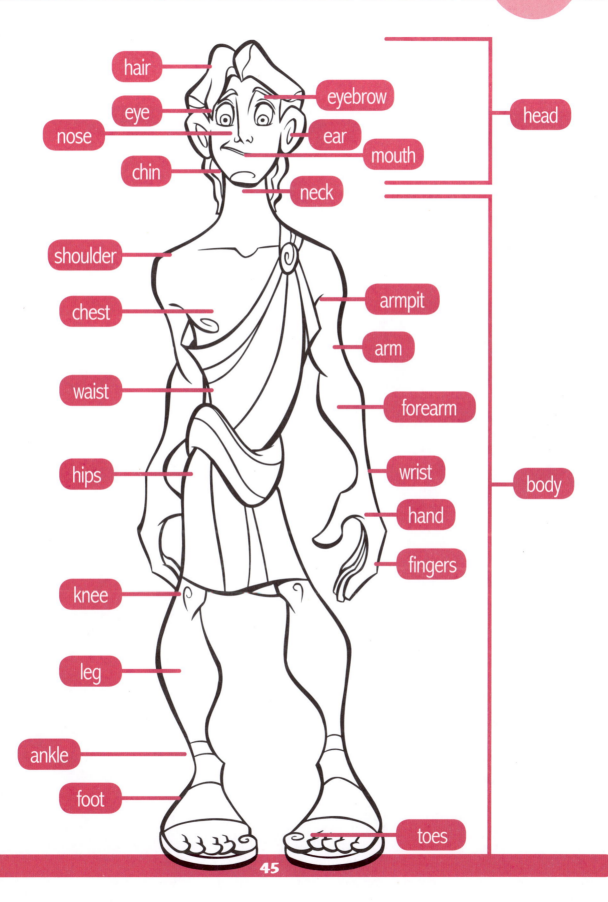

18 Nature

rainbow

clouds

tree

mushroom

water drops

fire

moon

sun

rain

spiderweb

flowers

46

wave

bubbles

rose

mountain

waterfall

pine tree

hill

leaf

island

river

beach

19 Vehicles

trailer

dump truck

 crane truck

scooter

fire truck

sailboat

hot air balloon

helicopter

motorcycle

propeller plane

blimp

double decker bus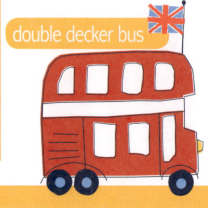

48

space ship

cement mixer

bulldozer

tire

taxi cab

racing car

carriage

tow truck

buggy

convertible

bicycle

hydroplane

tractor

airplane

steam train

49

20 Seasons

Spring

Summer

Fall

Winter

Solar System 21

The Sun

Venus

Jupiter

Mercury

Earth

Mars

Uranus

Saturn

Neptune

Pluto
(dwarf planet)

22 What Are You Doing?

listening to music

talking on the phone

dancing

taking a bath

hugging

flying

sleeping

winking

playing the piano

giving the baby a bath

dancing

holding hands

riding on a magic carpet

eating ice cream

smelling a flower

holding a book

running

looking in the mirror

being in nature

riding a horse

23 Countries Of The World

Asia

| SOUTH KOREA | INDIA | JAPAN | CHINA | KYRGYZSTAN | VIETNAM | CAMBODIA |

| SAUDI ARABIA | IRAQ | LEBANON | UNITED ARAB EMIRATES | SYRIA | ISRAEL | IRAN |

Americas

| ARGENTINA | CUBA | BRAZIL | USA | CANADA | URUGUAY | COLOMBIA |

| PERU | ECUADOR | CHILE | DOMINICAN REPUBLIC | VENEZUELA | MEXICO |

Africa

| SOUTH AFRICA | EGYPT | CAMEROON | NIGERIA | REPUBLIC OF THE CONGO | ALGERIA | UGANDA |

| LIBERIA | ZIMBABWE | SENEGAL | ZAMBIA | CÔTE D'IVOIRE | RWANDA | MOZAMBIQUE |

Europe

| FRANCE | SWEDEN | GREECE | SPAIN | FINLAND | IRELAND | ITALY |

| SWITZERLAND | RUSSIA | ICELAND | NETHERLANDS | POLAND | UNITED KINGDOM | PORTUGAL |

Oceania

| AUSTRALIA | TONGA |

Antarctica

ANTARCTICA

| SOLOMON ISLANDS | NEW ZEALAND |

24 Emotions

furious

 suspicious

 excited

angry

 peaceful

 brave

tired

bored

sleepy

 afraid

 curious

scared

 fancy

 worried

 amazed

 happy

absorbed

 confident

 sad

 serious

shy

confident

surprised

proud

disgusted

intrigued

25 Alphabet

A <ei>

B <bi>

C <ci>

D <di>

E <i>

F <éf>

G <dji>

H <eidj>

I <ái>

<djei>   <kei>   <él>

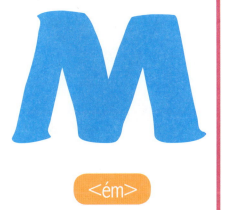  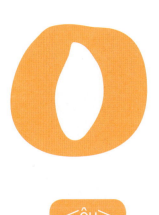

<ém>   <én>   <ôu>

<pí>   <quiú>   <ár>

25 Alphabet

S	T	U
<éss>	<tí>	<iú>

V	W	X
<vi>	<dãbou iú>	<écss>

Y	Z	
<uái>	<zi>	

60

Numbers 26

0	1	2	3	4	5	6
zero	one	two	three	four	five	six

7	8	9	10	11	12	13
seven	eight	nine	ten	eleven	twelve	thirteen

14	15	16	17	18	19	20
fourteen	fifteen	sixteen	seventeen	eighteen	nineteen	twenty

21	22	23	24	25	26	27
twenty-one	twenty-two	twenty-three	twenty-four	twenty-five	twenty-six	twenty-seven

28	29	30	40	50	60	70
twenty-eight	twenty-nine	thirty	forty	fifty	sixty	seventy

80	90	100	1000
eighty	ninety	one hundred	one thousand

1000000 — one million

61

27 Days Of The Week

JANUARY

Monday	Tuesday	Wednesday	Thursday	Friday	Saturday	Sunday
M	T	W	T	F	S	S
1	2	3	4	5	6	7
8	9	10	11	12	13	14
15	16	17	18	19	20	21
22	23	24	25	26	27	28
29	30	31				

Months Of The Year 28

January
M	T	W	T	F	S	S
1	2	3	4	5	6	7
8	9	10	11	12	13	14
15	16	17	18	19	20	21
22	23	24	25	26	27	28
29	30	31				

February
M	T	W	T	F	S	S
			1	2	3	4
5	6	7	8	9	10	11
12	13	14	15	16	17	18
19	20	21	22	23	24	25
26	27	28				

March
M	T	W	T	F	S	S
			1	2	3	4
5	6	7	8	9	10	11
12	13	14	15	16	17	18
19	20	21	22	23	24	25
26	27	28	29	30	31	

April
M	T	W	T	F	S	S
						1
2	3	4	5	6	7	8
9	10	11	12	13	14	15
16	17	18	19	20	21	22
23	24	25	26	27	28	29
30						

May
M	T	W	T	F	S	S
	1	2	3	4	5	6
7	8	9	10	11	12	13
14	15	16	17	18	19	20
21	22	23	24	25	26	27
28	29	30	31			

June
M	T	W	T	F	S	S
				1	2	3
4	5	6	7	8	9	10
11	12	13	14	15	16	17
18	19	20	21	22	23	24
25	26	27	28	29	30	

July
M	T	W	T	F	S	S
						1
2	3	4	5	6	7	8
9	10	11	12	13	14	15
16	17	18	19	20	21	22
23	24	25	26	27	28	29
30	31					

August
M	T	W	T	F	S	S
	1	2	3	4	5	
6	7	8	9	10	11	12
13	14	15	16	17	18	19
20	21	22	23	24	25	26
27	28	29	30	31		

September
M	T	W	T	F	S	S
					1	2
3	4	5	6	7	8	9
10	11	12	13	14	15	16
17	18	19	20	21	22	23
24	25	26	27	28	29	30

October
M	T	W	T	F	S	S
1	2	3	4	5	6	7
8	9	10	11	12	13	14
15	16	17	18	19	20	21
22	23	24	25	26	27	28
29	30	31				

November
M	T	W	T	F	S	S
			1	2	3	4
5	6	7	8	9	10	11
12	13	14	15	16	17	18
19	20	21	22	23	24	25
26	27	28	29	30		

December
M	T	W	T	F	S	S
					1	2
3	4	5	6	7	8	9
10	11	12	13	14	15	16
17	18	19	20	21	22	23
24	25	26	27	28	29	30
31						

I ♥ minnie

29 My New Words

Here is a place to write down all the new English words you find!

(Escreva aqui todas as novas palavras em Inglês que você descobrir!)